This book is a gift to

. . . . . . . . . . . . . . . . . . . . . . . . . . . . . . . . . . . . . . . . . . . . . . . . . . . . . . . . . . . . . . . .

On the occasion of

. . . . . . . . . . . . . . . . . . . . . . . . . . . . . . . . . . . . . . . . . . . . . . . . . . . . . . . . . . . . . . . .

Date

. . . . . . . . . . . . . . . . . . . . . . . . . . . . . . . . . . . . . . . . . . . . . . . . . . . . . . . . . . . . . . . .

From

. . . . . . . . . . . . . . . . . . . . . . . . . . . . . . . . . . . . . . . . . . . . . . . . . . . . . . . . . . . . . . . .

# A Christening Gift

## Prayer and Memory Book

ILLUSTRATED BY MIQUE MORIUCHI

lion cub
books

May my life shine
like a star in the night,
filling my world with
goodness and light.

Based on Philippians,
chapter 2, verse 15

# All About Me

My name is

..............................................................................

I was born on

..............................................................................

at

..............................................................................

6

Photo of me

As I grow, I learn to do new things.
These are my first achievements

(     months)
....................................................................

(     months)
....................................................................

(     months)
....................................................................

(     months)
....................................................................

Photo of me playing

Before I was made,
God loved me.

When I was born,
God loved me.

Now I am here,
God loves me.

For ever and ever,
God loves me.

Dear God,
You know all about me.
You created me inside and out.
I am beautifully and wonderfully made.
You know all my days ahead and
you will keep me safe.

Based on Psalm 139

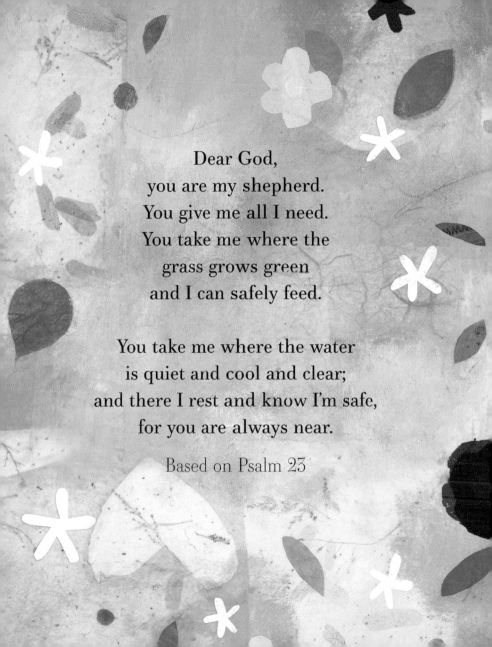

Dear God,
you are my shepherd.
You give me all I need.
You take me where the
grass grows green
and I can safely feed.

You take me where the water
is quiet and cool and clear;
and there I rest and know I'm safe,
for you are always near.

Based on Psalm 23

# My Family

The people in my family are

........................................................

........................................................

........................................................

We live

........................................................

........................................................

........................................................

Photo showing me
with my family

# Special Moments
# With My Family

Photo of special moment

............................................. (date)

Photo of special moment

............................................... (date)

O God,
As truly as you are our father,
so, just as truly, you are our mother.
We thank you, God our father,
for your strength and goodness.
We thank you, God our mother,
for the closeness of your caring.
O God, we thank you for the great love
you have for each one of us.

Based on a reflection by
Julian of Norwich (1312–c. 1416)

People were also bringing babies to
Jesus for him to place his hands on them.
When the disciples saw this, they turned
them away. But Jesus called the children
to him and said, "Let the little children
come to me, and do not stop them.
The kingdom of God belongs to them."

Based on Luke, chapter 18, verses 15 and 16

Jesus, friend of little children,
be a friend to me;
take my hand, and ever keep me
close to thee.

Walter John Mathams (1853–1931)

Thank you, God,
that the circle of my family and friends
is safe within the circle of your love,
which never ends.

# My Special Day

Celebrations are filled with joy and
happiness and shared with one another.

The guests who came to my special day were

...........................................................

...........................................................

...........................................................

...........................................................

...........................................................

The invitation

Photo of my special day

Photo of my special day

Praise the Lord from heaven,
all beings of the height!
Praise him, holy angels
and golden sun so bright.
Praise him, silver moonlight,
praise him, every star!
Let your praises shine
throughout the universe so far.
Praise the Lord from earth below,
all beings of the deep!

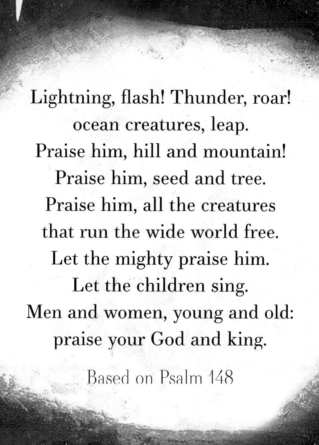

Lightning, flash! Thunder, roar!
ocean creatures, leap.
Praise him, hill and mountain!
Praise him, seed and tree.
Praise him, all the creatures
that run the wide world free.
Let the mighty praise him.
Let the children sing.
Men and women, young and old:
praise your God and king.

Based on Psalm 148

Jesus said . . .
"I am the light of the world.
Whoever follows me will never walk in
darkness, but will have the light of life."

John, chapter 8, verse 12

Jesus said . . .
"A new command I give you:
love one another. As I have loved you,
so you must love one another."

John, chapter 13, verse 34

We can do no great things,
only small things with great love.

Mother Teresa of Calcutta (1910–1997)

Christ be with me,
Christ within me,
Christ behind me,
Christ before me,
Christ beside me,
Christ to win me,
Christ to comfort and restore me,
Christ beneath me,
Christ above me,
Christ in quiet and
Christ in danger,
Christ in hearts of all that love me,
Christ in mouth of friend and stranger.

St Patrick (389–461)

# My Special Prayers

Special prayers and promises
from those who love me

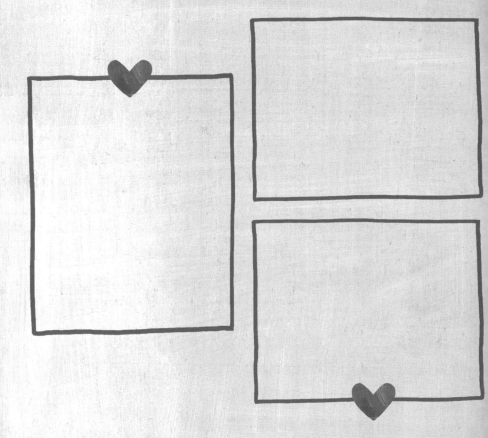

One day, when Jesus had finished praying,
one of his disciples said to him,
"Lord, teach us to pray".

Jesus gave them this prayer:

Our Father in heaven,
hallowed be your name,
your kingdom come,
your will be done,
on earth as in heaven.
Give us today our daily bread.
Forgive us our sins
as we forgive those who sin against us.
Lead us not into temptation
but deliver us from evil.
For the kingdom, the power
and the glory are yours
now and for ever.
Amen.

Jesus said . . .
"Ask, and you will receive;
seek, and you will find;
knock, and the door
will be opened to you.

"Your Father in heaven
will give good things
to those who ask him."

Based on Matthew,
chapter 7, verses 7 and 11

God is our shelter and strength,
always ready to help in times of trouble.
So we will not be afraid,
even if the earth is shaken
and mountains fall into the ocean depths;
even if the seas roar and rage,
and the hills are shaken.
God is with us;
God is our fortress.

Based on Psalm 46, verses 1 to 3 and 7

# My Church Family

I was welcomed at

. . . . . . . . . . . . . . . . . . . . . . . . . . . . . . . . . . . . . . . . . . . . . . . . . . . . . . . .

led by

. . . . . . . . . . . . . . . . . . . . . . . . . . . . . . . . . . . . . . . . . . . . . . . . . . . . . . . .

Photo of the
church or venue

Dear God,
Shelter me in the
kingdom of your love.

Jesus said,
"Listen! The kingdom of heaven
is like a mustard seed, which a
farmer plants in his field.
Although it is the smallest of
all seeds, when it grows,
it becomes a tall tree.
All the birds come and perch
in its branches."

Based on Matthew, chapter 13,
verses 31 and 32

Jesus said,
"Listen! The only thing that really
matters is being part of God's kingdom.
Don't worry about anything else.

"Look at the wild birds. They don't
worry about sowing seeds or gathering
a harvest. They know that God
will take care of them.

"Look at the wild flowers. They don't
worry about making clothes. God gives
them petals that are far more beautiful
than the most expensive clothes.

"If God cares so much about the birds
and flowers, you can be sure that God
will take even more care of you."

Based on Matthew, chapter 6,
verses 25 to 34

Love is giving, not taking,
mending, not breaking,
trusting, believing,
never deceiving,
patiently bearing
and faithfully sharing
each joy, each sorrow,
today and tomorrow.

# Blessings For Me

Special messages, words of
encouragement, and blessings for me

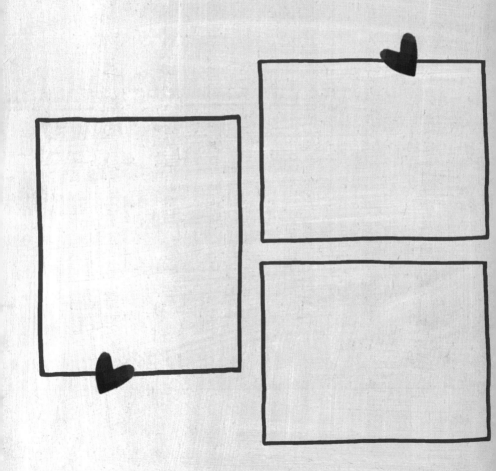

May God bless you and
take care of you.
May God be kind to you and
do good things for you.
May God look on you with love
and give you peace.

Based on Numbers, chapter 6,
verses 24 to 26

Deep peace of the
running waves to you,
deep peace of the
flowing air to you,
deep peace of the
quiet earth to you,
deep peace of the
shining stars to you,
deep peace of the
shade of night to you,
moon and stars always
giving light to you,
deep peace of Christ,
the Son of Peace, to you.

Traditional Gaelic blessing

Spirit of God
put love in my life.
Spirit of God
put joy in my life.
Spirit of God
put peace in my life.
Spirit of God
make me patient.
Spirit of God
make me kind.

Spirit of God
make me good.
Spirit of God
give me faithfulness.
Spirit of God
give me humility.
Spirit of God
give me self-control.

Based on Galatians, chapter 5,
verses 22 to 23

May the grace of the Lord Jesus
be with everyone.
Amen.

Based on Revelation, chapter 22,
verse 21 – the last line of the Bible

Published by **Lion Cub Books**
Part of the SPCK Group
SPCK, Studio 101, The Record Hall,
16–16A Baldwin's Gardens, London EC1N 7RJ

ISBN 978-1-915748-04-1

First edition 2024

**Acknowledgments**

Scripture quotations taken from The Holy Bible, New International Version® NIV®
Copyright © 1973 1978 1984 2011 by Biblica, Inc. TM
Used by permission. All rights reserved worldwide.

The Lord's Prayer (page 38) copyright © The English Language Liturgical Consultation and is reproduced by permission of the publisher.

Unattributed prayers and verses compiled and written by Sophie Piper and Lois Rock

A catalogue record for this book is available from the British Library

Produced on paper from sustainable sources

Printed and bound in China, October 2023 by Dream Colour (Hong Kong) Printing Limited